A
Handbook
for
Today's Disciples

in the Christian Church
(Disciples of Christ)
Revised Edition

D. Duane Cummins

Chalice Press.
St. Louis, Missouri

All scripture quotations, unless otherwise indicated, are from the *New Revised Standard Version Bible*, copyright 1989, Division of Christian Education of the National Council of the Churches of Christ in the USA. Used by permission.

Scripture quotations marked (NEB) are from *The New English Bible*, copyright Oxford University Press and Cambridge University Press 1961, 1970. Reprinted by permission.

Visit Chalice Press on the World Wide Web at
www.chalicepress.com

12 11 10 9   00 01 02 03 04 05

Library of Congress Cataloging-in-Publication Data
Cummins, D. Duane.
A handbook for today's Disciples.
1. Christian Church (Disciples of Christ)
I. Title
BX7321.2.C85   1991   286.6'3   81-10029
ISBN 0-8272-1425-1   AACR2

Printed in the United States of America

TO
SUZI

Companion in Faith
Partner in Life

Acknowledgments

Preparation of this second edition adds indebtedness to many fine persons.

To Lawrence S. Steinmetz and Frank Helms, I express deep gratitude for their caring research assistance.

To Ronald E. Osborn and Clark Williamson, I extend abiding appreciation for their thoughtful reading and insightful criticisms.

To Jim Suggs and David Polk for their support of the publication of this new edition, I am heavily indebted.

To Margaret Stewart and Sherry Tallman who patiently transcribed the final manuscript on word processors, I express genuine appreciation.

D. Duane Cummins
Bethany College
January 1, 1991

Contents

Introduction

A *Handbook for Today's Disciples* has been prepared to help present-day church members understand the heritage, mission, thought, worship, and structure of the Christian Church (Disciples of Christ). It is designed for many uses: as (1) an overview for new members, (2) an updated briefing for veteran members, (3) a synopsis for the casual reader, and (4) a summary guide for study courses on the Christian Church (Disciples of Christ).

The chapters of this volume stand separately. The reader may arrange them in any order and consider them in any sequence desired. Readers unfamiliar with Disciples history should begin with Chapter One, "The Disciples: A Historical Sketch," because it establishes the context within which all subsequent chapters are more easily understood. Those who know the heritage may begin reading wherever they choose.

In the pages that follow, you will discover a profound sense of mission unique in the annals of religion, a fierce devotion to the integrity of individual choice, and an extraordinary strength of faith. It is a grand legacy. It is a Disciples legacy, one to be read and cherished.

1

The Disciples: A Historical Sketch

This is a story with many names—"An American Religious Movement," "The Second Reformation," "The Restoration Movement," "An Experiment in Liberty," "Reformation for Christian Unity"—each offering added dimension to the richly varied personality of the subject. This is the story of the Christian Church (Disciples of Christ).

Lines of thought and spirit that give shape to the story extend from distant places in distant times and from nearby in the recent past. They extend from first-century Antioch and Corinth; from eighteenth-century Glasgow and County Down; from nineteenth-century Bethany and Cane Ridge; and from a new land known as the "workshop of liberty," recognized for its egalitarian voice, its pragmatic thought, and its enormous belief in the worth and capacity of the individual. These many lines of genesis fashioned the basic instincts and intuitions of the Christian Church (Disciples of Christ).

1804/09—1830: Conception

By 1800, the tumult of the American Revolution was receding in time and with it a winter season in the annals of

American religion. A new religious revivalism surged across the land, challenging institutional religion and calling for a return to the New Testament church. In due course, the new revivalism blended with the frontiering process, following its natural way of establishing religion as the next level of social organization above the family.

The frontier, always a fertile field for social and cultural experiment, became a virtual seedbed for new religious sects, factions, and beliefs. Self-reliant frontier settlers sought a brand of Christianity that mirrored their own character: individualistic, uncomplicated, free of corporate authority, and unbound by tradition. The formalized church of the time did not offer such characteristics and became irrelevant to the frontier settlers. The simple, practical, and independent religious movements spawned by the new revivalism captured the spirit of the early pioneers

Deep in the summer of 1801, a celebrated revival at Cane Ridge, hosted by the soulful Barton W. Stone, a Presbyterian minister in Bourbon County, Kentucky, set the tone of religious evangelism for a century and beyond. Presbyterian authorities, shocked by the disregard for doctrine, the absence of denominational distinctions, and the spirited behavior of many Cane Ridge participants, aired a blistering criticism that led to the formation of a splinter presbytery. On June 28, 1804, Barton Stone and his five colleagues who formed the new presbytery issued a landmark document in the history of religious liberty entitled, *The Last Will and Testament of the Springfield Presbytery*. It flatly dissolved their new organization. The reformers in this unprecedented defiance of authority refused recognition of any organization above the congregation. They pointed to the scriptures as their single source of authority, and they proclaimed union with all believers in Christ through their expressed intent to "sink into union with the Body of Christ." This autonomous group of reformers, fostered by Barton Stone, took for itself the name *Christians*. Its popular advocacy of independence, simplicity, and practicality attracted a determined following of frontier folk.

Similar seeds of reform had been planted among Methodists in Virginia by James O'Kelly and among Baptists in New Hampshire by Elias Smith, before reaching the Presbyterians of Kentucky. The seeds of reform also spread to the hill country of western Pennsylvania, where Thomas Campbell, a scholarly Scotch-Irish minister, immigrated in 1807. He came to the Allegheny wilderness wearied by the fragmentation of the Presbyterian church in his native islands, and he came driven by the impulse to reform. Soon in contention with Presbyterian authorities in America, he organized the nondenominational Christian Association of Washington, Pennsylvania. On September 7, 1809, Campbell released his famous *Declaration and Address*, destined to become chart and compass for the entire movement. No other document equals its influence upon the Christian Church (Disciples of Christ). It contained thirteen propositions for the restoration of the principles of the New Testament church and for the realization of Christian union. The most widely recited of those propositions was the first: "That the church of Christ upon earth is essentially, intentionally and constitutionally one."

Within weeks of the document's publication, Thomas Campbell's twenty-one-year-old son, Alexander, arrived in America. Fresh from his university studies at Glasgow, Alexander found himself in full accord with the call of reform in the Declaration, and quickly discarded much of his Glasgow experience. He soon displaced his father as leader of the tiny community of reformers. The Christian Association reconstituted itself as the Brush Run Church in 1811, adopting a scriptural format of the "ancient order of things." This format included several New Testament precepts:

- Christ, the bedrock of their faith and head of the church.
- The Bible, sole authority, with emphasis on the New Testament.
- Baptism by immersion and for responsible believers.

- The Lord's Supper, celebrated weekly.

- Government, vested in congregational leadership, with no distinction between clergy and laity.

The Brush Run congregation was loosely federated with the Redstone Association of Baptists. On August 30, 1816, Alexander Campbell delivered his now celebrated *Sermon on the Law* at Cross Creek, boldly proclaiming that Christians lived under grace, not law; under Christ, not Moses; under the New Testament, not the Old. This breach of Baptist doctrine brought the Brush Run reformers abrupt dismissal from the Redstone Association. Untroubled, the little congregation continued its life in associational relationship with the neighboring Mahoning Baptist Association, where it had joined before the Redstone dismissal.

During the crowded years of the 1820s, the Stone and Campbell movements broke out of the geographic provincialism that had stunted their respective reforms. Following a decade of largely unnoticed labor, Alexander Campbell engaged in a series of widely publicized debates, published a Christian hymnal, along with a modern version of the New Testament, and inaugurated the circulation of a periodical, *The Christian Baptist.* Stone published a periodical of his own, *The Christian Messenger,* and opened an acquaintance with Campbell. Late in the decade, Walter Scott, another newly arrived Scottish Highlander, began work as an evangelist for the Mahoning Association, to promote the restoration movement. Through a practical and high-voltage appeal, the "Voice of the Golden Oracle" won thousands of former Baptists to the reform and earned status as one of the central figures of the movement. Scott's extraordinary evangelism unlocked the parochial shackles and gave the movement its freedom to grow.

Ousting Campbell-Scott reformers from Baptist associations became common sport. The action at Austintown, Ohio, in 1830, when the Mahoning Baptist Association voted to dissolve itself, was a matter of consequence. Although the Brush Run reformers and the Baptists could not achieve harmonious consensus on the issues of faith and polity, the dissolution was still unexpected. The event is recognized as a milestone in the history of the reform movement. From that moment, the reformers were clearly independent, no longer functioning in association with an established denomination, and henceforward distinctively identified as Disciples, rather than Baptists. It was the moment of birth.

1830—1866: The Infant Years

The Millennial Harbinger, authored and edited by Alexander Campbell, appeared in 1830, replacing the former *Christian Baptist.* The *Harbinger,* more temperate toward the need for church structure, carried hints of an awakening sense of social responsibility in Campbell's thinking, helping to ease the way for eventual union with the movement initiated by Barton Stone. Despite his testy editorial exchanges with the more conciliatory Stone, Campbell supported the idea of union between their kindred groups, an idea transformed into fact on January 1, 1832, at Hill Street Christian Church in Lexington, Kentucky.

Disciples and *Christians* launched the delicate process of becoming one. They found common ground in rejecting human creeds, accepting the centrality of Christ in their faith, recognizing the supreme authority of scripture, and proclaiming their mutual desire for union. The matters of evangelism, concepts of ministry, frequency of communion, and form of baptism resisted resolution. The more substantive issues of balancing liberty and order, and faith and reason, remained in creative tension. Irresolutions remained on the lesser question of an appropriate name. Campbell insisted upon the use of *Disciples* as a more historic, scriptural, and descriptive identification. Stone was equally insistent upon the use of *Christians,* the term tending to prevail in the names of congregations.

Growth characterized the decades of this period. Union, achieved congregation by congregation during the early thirties, joined some ten thousand Christians and twelve thousand Disciples. Reaching out from its regional base, the Stone-Campbell reform soon spanned the continent. During the 1830s, new congregations took root in Detroit, Baltimore, Dubuque, and Little Rock; in Brownville, Nebraska, and Bowie County, Texas; in Indiana, Illinois, and Missouri. The California and Oregon trails carried scores of "Campbellites" to the far West during the overland migrations of the forties and fifties. By 1860, the movement exhibited national proportions, with a membership of nearly 200,000 in 2100 congregations. Yet it achieved relatively little headway east of the Alleghenies, especially in New York and New England.

Order was the theme of the 1840s. Prompted by the demand for informed and responsible leadership within the congregations of the rapidly expanding movement, Alexander Campbell published a second edition of his compendium of Disciples beliefs, *The Christian System*, and donated land upon which he founded Bethany College for the purpose of formally educating a cadre of laity. Attempting to develop a structured means of cooperation among the many congregations, Campbell initiated a decade-long series of articles in the *Harbinger* on the controversial subject of church organization. The founding of the American Christian Bible Society in 1845 represented the earliest attempt to design a general structure.

By 1840, members of some congregations had begun to gather for fellowship in state "conventions," and, in 1849, the first national gathering of the movement convened in Cincinnati, with 156 delegates from one hundred churches in eleven states. The convention approved the formation of the American Christian Missionary Society in the hope of achieving a greater sense of national cooperation and international vision. While the creation of a structure beyond the congregation stirred opposition among those who thought such a structure violated a basic principle of the movement, it was welcomed by others as a much-delayed recognition of corporate responsibility for a larger mission.

Confrontation with the peculiar institution of slavery persuaded the reformers to seek a nondivisive position. They were led to the notion that the issue was a matter of "opinion," not "faith," and therefore was not a test of fellowship. While most mainline denominations were structurally fractured by the economic, social, and political devastation of the Civil War, Disciples forestalled that fate because of their inherent organizational elasticity and their commitment to the freedom of individual choice. Fissure remained below the surface and, with the death of Alexander Campbell on March 4, 1866, a new generation was left to struggle for internal repair.

1866—1917: Years of Adolescence

The founders were in their graves. Barton Stone died in 1844, Thomas Campbell in 1854, Walter Scott in 1861, and Alexander Campbell in 1866. Still under the rule of its two-fold plea to restore the ancient order and to build Christian unity, the movement entered upon a new forty-year journey, marked by dramatic numerical growth, budding denominational consciousness, and deepening internal division of thought.

A choice of direction inevitably confronts the second generation of all reforms. The Stone-Campbell movement had to decide if it should cement the views of the founders and hold solidly to traditions of the old order; or if it should venture into intellectual freshness, change, and flexibility, and adapt its ministry to the newly emerging socio-cultural-economic environment of post-Civil War America. Choosing between these two directions was compounded by the lingering bitterness of the Civil War and the profound paradox of the two-fold plea. The leaders, lacking the personal force of the founders, were not able to consolidate the membership. Part of the movement veered one direction, part of it went the other way, and they were never reconciled.

The surface battles within the movement were fought on the issues of the New Testament forbidding or permitting the use of instrumental music in worship, the organization of missionary societies beyond the congregation, and the development of a professional ministry with title and authority. The battles raged for forty years, but in the end, it was the deeper dissension that severed the relationship. The Churches of Christ, concentrated in the former Confederate states, followed the first path in pursuit of the ancient order. The Disciples of Christ, concentrated in the upper Midwest, followed the second in pursuit of Christian unity. The initial separate listing of the two groups in the 1906 Federal Religious Census was little more than a statistical event, since their choice of separate ways had long since been made.

Between the Civil War and World War I, four important ministries grew out of Disciples vision. The first was journalism. Always abundant in editors, the Disciples were particularly fortunate to be influenced in this period by the progressive insights of Isaac Errett, editor of the *Christian-Standard*, and J.H. Garrison, editor of *The Christian Evangelist*, a weekly periodical now replaced by a monthly called *The Disciple*. The second ministry was a pioneering missionary initiative, parented by the leadership of Caroline Neville Pearre and Archibald McLean. The formation of the Christian Woman's Board of Missions and the Foreign Christian Missionary Society in 1874-75, coupled with the development of the National Benevolent Association in 1877, provided a means of outreach and contact with the larger world. The third ministry was higher education. Disciples reactivated the long religious tradition of intellectual leadership that the new revivalism had abandoned. The founding and developing of more than four hundred Disciples-related educational institutions produced a more informed laity, and educators soon exercised considerable influence upon the thought and practice of the movement. The fourth ministry was cooperation with other communions. Disciples were charter members of the Federal Council of Churches, and, due to the creative foresight of Peter Ainslie, originated the Council on Christian Union in 1910. These four ministries continue to enliven and enlarge Disciples vision.

While these four activities were invaluable in stretching late nineteenth-century Disciples thought, they were not able to overcome the cultural and intellectual limitations of a rural confinement or successfully bridge the chasm between church and society. Consequently the movement, like much of American Protestantism, was not adequately prepared to address the new social heterogeneity, to attempt assimilation of the growing tides of immigrants, to adjust to the rapidly developing urban-industrial complex, or to hear the public distress over social ethics, poverty, and a host of related issues. It remained essentially a rural, county-seat-town movement.

When the Disciples celebrated the centennial of the Declaration and Address in 1909, they numbered 1,250,000 members, largely the result of their effective evangelism. In spite of division and cultural isolation, they enjoyed phenomenal growth, but the "restoration of the ancient order" became a more elusive goal in the new socioeconomic order.

1917—1968: Drive to Maturity

By the end of the First World War, the bone and sinew of the movement were in place. With their physical growth stabilized, Disciples entered a time of intellectual refinement and structural consolidation.

The most telling influence upon Disciples during these years came from a new theology advocating thorough historical research of the scriptures and an intellectual awareness of contemporary cultural trends. After many years of controversy between the "new liberals" and the orthodox defenders of an insulated biblicism, the exponents of each view locked in open rivalry for control of the College of the Bible at Lexington, Kentucky. The outcome of the 1917 hearings, which amounted to a heresy trial, established the new theology as the predominant intellectual force among Disciples for the next forty years. Among the effects of this theological shift was a waning of the concept of unchanging applicability and demand of New Testament precedents and a release from the tunnel vision of the one-hundred-year effort to "restore the ancient order." Exemplars of this new theological position—Herbert L. Willett, Edward Scribner Ames, Winfred E. Garrison, and Charles Clayton Morrison—were among the influential architects of Disciples thought during the first half of the twentieth century.

An additional consequence of the controversy was the gradual withdrawal from fellowship with Disciples by those who thought the Stone-Campbell movement had forsaken its heritage. This group eventually numbered 650,000 members and moved to final separation during the days of discord surrounding "restructure" in the late 1960s. Separation actually began at the time of the 1926 International Convention in Memphis—with a rump convention in the Pantages Theater, where the North American Christian Convention first organized—and ultimately concluded with a separate 1971 yearbook listing for the Christian Churches and Churches of Christ.

The unending search for more efficient organization led to the International Convention of the Disciples of Christ, established in 1917. Likewise, the United Christian Missionary Society was created in 1920, unifying six independent boards into a single church agency. These reconstituted organizations served Disciples ministry through the acculturation of the 1920s, the economic depression of the 1930s, and the Second World War in the 1940s. Many other agencies and committees were developed along the way. The most widely known grew out of the fellowship concept and included the Christian Youth Fellowship (1944), the Christian Women's Fellowship (1949), and the Christian Men's Fellowship (1951).

The post-World War II proliferation of organized agencies within the movement produced confusion. Near the end of the 1950s, a Panel of Scholars, composed of many of the finest Disciples minds, was commissioned to reexamine Disciples precepts in light of the new religious vitality of that day. The Panel report, completed and published in the early sixties, softened the old rigidities of Disciples thought on theology and church structure. Simultaneously, the International Convention, meeting in 1960 in Louisville, Kentucky, brought into existence the Commission on Brotherhood Restructure, directing it to create a new form of organization rooted in something more substantive than a simple coalition of autonomous agencies, fellowships, congregations, committees, and conventions. The Restructure Commission, under the imaginative leadership of Granville T. Walker, A. Dale Fiers, and Kenneth L. Teegarden, labored throughout the religiously disillusioned sixties forging a unique covenantal design. The Provisional Design for the Christian Church (Disciples of Christ) was approved overwhelmingly by a representative Assembly meeting at Kansas City in 1968.

Since 1968: Maturity

Approval of the Provisional Design marked the passage of Disciples into denominational maturity. Officially named the Christian Church (Disciples of Christ), they became a church.

The genius of the design was lodged in the concept of covenant. Through covenant, the congregations, regions, and general agencies were linked in an interdependent and mutually supportive relationship, working in concert, none the mere servant of the other, all accountable to each other. Through covenant, the church was able to occasion a more equitable balance between some of its ageless polarities— "freedom and community," "unity and diversity," "congregationalism and catholicity." Through covenant, the church was able to minister more effectively to a post-industrial society and to pursue more confidently its venerable goal of Christian unity.

The new covenantal design entered a ten-year period of implementation culminating in 1977 with the removal of the term *provisional* from the Design and the decision to proceed without the writing of a formal constitution. A. Dale Fiers, elected the first General Minister and President (1968-1973) of the restructured church, was succeeded by Kenneth L. Teegarden (1973-1985) and John O. Humbert (1985-1991). Membership in the Christian Church (Disciples of Christ) numbered just over one million in 1990. The mutual affinity and pervasive bond among these tens of thousands is expressed through covenant, entered voluntarily and in love.

Disciples Affirmations

The name of this body shall be CHRISTIAN CHURCH (DISCIPLES OF CHRIST).

Within the universal body of Christ, the Christian Church (Disciples of Christ) in the United States of America and in Canada is identifiable by its tradition, name, institutions and relationships. Across national boundaries this church expresses itself in free and voluntary relationships in congregational, regional and general manifestations.

The Design

Scriptures

It was in Antioch that the disciples were first called "Christians."

Acts 11:26

"This is the covenant that I will make...I will put my laws in their minds, and write them on their hearts, and I will be their God, and they shall be my people."

Hebrews 8:10

For this reason he is the mediator of a new covenant, so that those who are called may receive the promised eternal inheritance, because a death has occurred that redeems them from the transgressions under the first covenant.

Hebrews 9:15

Above all, clothe yourselves with love, which binds everything together in perfect harmony. And let the peace of Christ rule in your hearts, to which indeed you were called in the one body. And be thankful.

Colossians 3:14–15

2

Disciples and
Christian Thought

The Scriptures

General Briefing

Seated around evening campfires, gathered at village wells, and in a score of similar settings, the ancient Hebrews retold their long-cherished ancestral stories. Their religious faith was rooted in those bits of heritage, interpreted to their own experiences and preserved through oral tradition from generation to generation. Well after the development of an alphabet nineteen centuries before the birth of Christ, the ancient stories were slowly gathered from many clans and later compiled into written form known to us now as the Old Testament. The Old Testament is a thirty-nine-document collection of history, law, prophecy, poetry, and folklore, sifted through many ages of Hebrew history. It is a record of God revealed through the testimony of herdsmen, kings, prophets, and poets.

Throughout most of the first century, the life and ministry of Christ was transmitted orally. As those who knew Jesus grew old or were martyred, it became important to preserve their knowledge and experience in written form. Scattered samplings of the recorded thoughts of several apostles who nurtured the early church through its formative days were gradually collected, and in the second century consolidated into a single volume later known as the New Testament. This is a compilation of twenty-seven documents, including Gospels, pastoral letters, history, and poetic vision revealing God through the life of Jesus Christ.

Although the two testaments contain sixty-six separate works, written by a variety of authors at irregular points in time over a span of more than twelve hundred years, there is an organic unity binding the parts into an interdependent whole. Together, the testaments form the Bible, a human testimony of God's revelation. Across the past three hundred years the Bible has been the most comprehensively analyzed book in all of literature. Thorough scrutiny will continue, and always will bring enlightenment rather than weakness to the truth of the message because the discernment of truth is lodged in the Bible's underlying spirit rather than its literal events. It is not faith in the book that Christians hold, but faith in God as revealed through the book.

Disciples Traditions

Seated in crude frontier meetinghouses and gathered in forest clearings, the early Disciples dedicated themselves to hearing, reading, and studying scripture. Their religious faith and vision of a restored church were solidly rooted in the New Testament, with particular reference to the book of Acts. Barton Stone believed that God worked through the testimony of scripture and that understanding the Bible was not dependent upon elaborate critical analysis. Alexander Campbell, however, believed that careful historical study of all biblical writings strengthened each believer's faith.

Disciples do not have an "official" interpretation of the Bible. Individuals are encouraged to interpret the scriptures in the light of all sciences and in the strength of Christian tradition. Because the Bible is viewed as human testimony of divine revelation, Disciples tend away from a literal approach and more toward an understanding that combines both faith and reason.

Disciples Affirmations

Where the scriptures speak, we speak; where the scriptures are silent, we are silent.

Sermon by Thomas Campbell, 1809

Within the universal church we receive...the light of scripture.

The Design

Scriptures

From childhood you have known the sacred writings that are able to instruct you for salvation through faith in Christ Jesus. All scripture is inspired by God and is useful for teaching, for reproof, for correction, and for training in righteousness, so that everyone who belongs to God may be proficient, equipped for every good work.

2 Timothy 3:15–17

So we have the prophetic message more fully confirmed. You will do well to be attentive to this as to a lamp shining in a dark place, until the day dawns and the morning star rises in your hearts.

2 Peter 1:19

We declare to you what was from the beginning, what we have heard, what we have seen with our eyes, what we have looked at and touched with our hands, concerning the word of life — this life was revealed, and we have seen it and testify to it, and declare to you the eternal life that was with the Father and was revealed to us — we declare to you what we have seen and heard so that you also may have fellowship with us; and truly our fellowship is with the Father and with his Son Jesus Christ. We are writing these things so that our joy may be complete.

I John 1:1–4

Since many have undertaken to set down an orderly account of the events that have been fulfilled among us, just as they were handed on to us by those who from the beginning were eyewitnesses and servants of the word, I too decided, after investigating everything carefully from the very first, to write an orderly account for you, most excellent Theophilus, so that you may know the truth concerning the things about which you have been instructed.

Luke 1:1–4

God

General Briefing

The first phrases of the Bible reveal God as Creator, an image reaffirmed in the poetic conviction of the psalmist. The Old Testament offers many intriguing concepts of God revealed through the history of Israel: a radiance in the desert of Midian; a giver of law on the slopes of Sinai; a deliverer of an enslaved people to freedom; a vindictive destroyer of civilization through the wrath of a great flood; a mysterious presence in a small wooden chest sojourning through the wilderness of Canaan; a force for justice, obedience, and righteousness; and a compassionate redeemer offering unrequited love to humankind. The conviction that God was actively at work in history held predominance throughout the development of Hebrew religious thought.

And the "word became flesh." In New Testament scripture the presence of God is intensely revealed through the person of Jesus Christ. That profound insight of God revealed in human life, the joining of divinity and humanity, sparked the extraordinary concept of individual contact with God as a personal relationship. The idea of a personal relationship between God and individuals and the idea of God as Creator are both embodied in the widely recited New Testament notion of the parental nature of God, a notion that continues to dominate Christian thought.

Disciples Traditions

Disciples, while not given to defining God, usually think of God as Creator and as revealed through the life of Jesus Christ. Many writers cite transcendent human attributes such as the sense of moral obligation, the capacity to appreciate beauty, the power to love, and the ability to know justice, honesty, mercy, and happiness as rational proofs of the existence of God in persons. Disciples do not reject reasonable evidences of God's existence but neither do they limit their understanding of God to rational definition. They view God as beyond definition, transcending time and geography, greater than all the energies shooting through nature, and more than a magnification of human powers. To reduce God solely to rational proof eliminates the role of faith. Disciples affirm the reality of God in the world but resist the temptation to enclose God in human definition. Barton Stone advised that true knowledge of God comes when by faith we receive "the testimony he has given of himself in his word."

Disciples Affirmations

We rejoice in God, maker of Heaven and Earth.

The Design

Scriptures

In the beginning when God created the heavens and the earth.

Genesis 1:1

In Christ God was reconciling the world to himself.

2 Corinthians 5:19

Dear friends, let us love one another, because love is from God. Everyone who loves is a child of God and knows God, but the unloving know nothing of God. For God is love.

1 John 4:7–8 (NEB)

"I AM WHO I AM....say to the Israelites, `The LORD, the God of your ancestors, the God of Abraham, the God of Isaac, and the God of Jacob, has sent me to you': This is my name forever, and this my title for all generations."

Exodus 3:14–15

In the beginning was the Word, and the Word was with God, and the Word was God. He was in the beginning with God. All things came into being through him, and without him not one thing came into being. What has come into being in him was life, and the life was the light of all people. And the Word became flesh and lived among us, and we have seen his glory, the glory as of a father's only son, full of grace and truth.

John 1:1–4,14

Jesus Christ

General Briefing

Jesus Christ was fully human, fully God. The historical circumstances of his life reveal the human Jesus. The presence of God in this person adds a dimension identified as the Christ, which we recognize and confess through faith. The joining of God with humanity in the person of Jesus Christ forms the very heart of the Christian faith. Although the question of Jesus Christ being divine or human or both confounds human wisdom, it is this union of humanity and divinity—the uniting of

the historical Jesus with the Christ of faith into a single being—
that expresses the fundamental claim of Christianity.

The historical Jesus is known to us through many sources.
Fragments of New Testament papyri recovered from the
sands of Mideastern deserts attest to the life of the human
Jesus. Chronicles of old, including the *Antiquities* of Josephus
(A.D. 93), the *Annals* of Tacitus (A.D. 110), and the *Lives of
the Twelve Caesars* by Suetonius (A.D. 98), all contain
historical references to Jesus.

The cold, historical facts of Jesus' human life can be
sketched in broad strokes. His earthly existence, beginning in
the days of Herod and ending in the time of Pilate, has been
fixed with relative accuracy. A carpenter by trade, his home-
town was the community of Nazareth in the province of
Galilee. During the final years of his brief life, a religious fervor
touched the Jordan Valley, drawing Jesus out of Nazareth and
into an extraordinary ministry. His contemporaries often
mistook his ministry as a political revolt, a misapprehension
that led to his arrest and execution.

It is the character rather than the biography of this man
that we know with thoroughness. He was called the *Christ*, a
Greek word meaning "the anointed one," or "the Messiah,"
the appointed one. The apostle Paul used the term again and
again in his many letters to describe the spiritual presence of
the risen Lord for a generation who had not known the human
Jesus in the flesh. The Gospels, written after the letters of Paul
and written specifically to proclaim the divinity of Christ, are
laden with anecdotes that reveal the depth of his divine
nature. Filled with the grace of God, Jesus performed unending
good works, turning all things base into things noble.

The very name "Jesus Christ" affirms that the historical
life was united with the grace of God. The human Jesus died
at the crucifixion, but the Christ of faith was resurrected. It is
this resurrection that provides for all generations the experience of faith in the Lord, Jesus Christ.

Disciples Traditions

"No Creed but Christ!" This phrase rings across the ages of Disciples history, heralding the belief that faith in Jesus Christ is a personal faith. Thomas and Alexander Campbell, along with Barton Stone, taught that creeds were irrelevant and that scripture alone was sufficient for faith in Jesus Christ.

The evolution of thought among Disciples regarding the humanity and divinity of Christ began with heavy emphasis upon the divine authority of the Christ of faith. Nineteenth-century preoccupation with the divinity of Christ caused the human Jesus to be generally ignored, but in the twentieth century Disciples thinking has experienced a steadily growing turn toward the life and teachings of the historical Jesus.

In our own time, Disciples have achieved a good balance in their thinking on the humanity and divinity of Jesus Christ. Disciples think of Jesus first as human, and then find in this individual the most complete, the most serene, the most thoroughly moral personality the world has ever known. His was a life "full of grace and truth." It is supremely the place in which we see God, not simply in the organization of the cosmos or in the moral order but in the mercy, the love, the compassion, the honesty, the will of Jesus Christ. Here is revealed God! The Christ of faith becomes a reality for all generations through the presence of God in Jesus. It brings us to confess gladly with those many generations before us that "Jesus is the Christ, the Son of the living God."

Disciples Affirmations

We confess that Jesus is the Christ, the Son of the living God, and proclaim him Lord and Savior of the world.

The Design

Scriptures

He said to them, "But who do you say that I am?" Simon Peter answered, "You are the Messiah, the Son of the living God."

And Jesus answered him, "Blessed are you, Simon son of Jonah! For flesh and blood has not revealed this to you, but my Father in heaven."

Matthew 16:15–17

And the Word became flesh and lived among us, and we have seen his glory, the glory as of a father's only son, full of grace and truth.

John 1:14

But these are written so that you may come to believe that Jesus is the Messiah, the Son of God, and that through believing you may have life in his name.

John 20:31

"Anyone who has seen me has seen the Father."

John 14:9 (NEB)

He is the image of the invisible God, the firstborn of all creation; for in him all things in heaven and on earth were created, things visible and invisible, whether thrones or dominions or rulers or powers — all things have been created through him and for him. He himself is before all things, and in him all things hold together. He is the head of the body, the church; he is the beginning, the firstborn from the dead, so that he might come to have first place in everything. For in him all the fullness of God was pleased to dwell, and through him God was pleased to reconcile to himself all things, whether on earth or in heaven, by making peace through the blood of his cross.

Colossians 1:15–20

The Holy Spirit

General Briefing

The search for the meaning of the Holy Spirit has continued throughout the entire history of Christianity. The prevailing view, common to several religious bodies, is that the Holy

Spirit is one member of a trinity co-existing with the Father and the Son in a single union. This view rests primarily on the writings of Paul, who explained that the Holy Spirit provides the means to understand the presence of the risen Christ in each believer and in the church. The Holy Spirit, in Paul's view, is separate from Christ, yet is the spirit of Christ, and it is the vehicle that unites the believer and the church with Christ. All Christians, stated Paul, who accept the gospel and are baptized will know the joy of the Spirit dwelling within them.

Paul was often called to elaborate upon his teaching about the Holy Spirit. The community of Christians at Galatia generally ignored any notion of spirit and drifted toward the legalistic doctrines of the past. Paul urged them to cultivate the sense of spirit; otherwise their religion would harden and die. By contrast, the community of Christians at Corinth carried the meaning of spirit to excess, which brought counsel from Paul to guard against developing a spiritually gifted elite and to understand that gifts such as prophecy and speaking in tongues were not exclusive as works of the spirit. From the earliest days of Christian history there have been multiple understandings of the Holy Spirit.

Disciples Traditions

Barton Stone defined the Holy Spirit as the "energy of God" and did not accept the idea that it was part of a trinity. He also believed that the Holy Spirit came to dwell in believers after they gained faith, not before.

Alexander Campbell advanced the rational view that the Holy Spirit speaks through the scriptures. It works through the scriptures and influences persons through words and ideas. In this way the Holy Spirit stimulates the church and molds the Christian character of individuals. While Campbell agreed with Stone that the Holy Spirit is given after faith rather than before, his definition of the Holy Spirit tended to create an identity apart from God or Christ and to see it as part of a divine unity.

These conflicting views have never been reconciled. In the 1880s Disciples thought continued the tradition that faith was necessary before the Holy Spirit could dwell within a believer. There was a growing feeling, however, that belief in a single method of receiving the Holy Spirit, only through the Word, was insufficient. Why wasn't everyone affected by the Word? Why couldn't the Holy Spirit work directly just as Satan supposedly did? Questions arose that accented the conflict of views and drew out the need for a faith that combined both the mind and the heart.

In the twentieth century, a great silence settled upon the Disciples search for meaning of the Holy Spirit. There has been very limited interest in the question, and Disciples theology has not developed any contemporary interpretation. The two views of Stone and Campbell still exist side by side, which says more about Disciples freedom of individual judgment and the unique ability to function as a church without theological conformity than it does about the Holy Spirit. The Christian Church (Disciples of Christ) in our time, therefore, encompasses both Galatia and Corinth, both Bethany and Cane Ridge. There are Disciples congregations unequivocally and sincerely committed to a charismatic faith expressed through gifts of the Holy Spirit including prophecy, speaking in tongues, and healing. There are also Disciples congregations that find their strength of spirit through liturgy, order, and historic tradition, to which they are committed with equal sincerity. The broad base of Discipledom is somewhere in between, yet all are seen as joined in a common covenant, with their sovereignty of individual choice undiminished.

Disciples Affirmations

In the communion of the Holy Spirit we are joined together in discipleship and in obedience to Christ.

The Design

Scriptures

...When we cry, "Abba! Father!" it is that very spirit bearing witness with our spirit that we are children of God, and if children, then heirs, heirs of God and joint heirs with Christ — if, in fact, we suffer with him so that we may also be glorified with him.

Romans 8:15–17

The only thing I want to learn from you is this: Did you receive the Spirit by doing the works of the law or by believing what you heard?

Galatians 3:2

The grace of the Lord Jesus Christ, the love of God, and the communion of the Holy Spirit be with all of you.

2 Corinthians 13:13

"...baptizing them in the name of the Father and of the Son and of the Holy Spirit....And remember, I am with you always, to the end of the age."

Matthew 28:19–20

3

Disciples and the Sacraments

Baptism

General Briefing

Somewhere between two Palestinian seas, Jesus stepped into the waters of the river Jordan and was baptized. Because that event marked the beginning of his ministry, it has frequently been interpreted as his ordination. With that seemingly simple act, Christ instituted a holy sacrament that, through two thousand years of practice, has grown complex in meaning and diverse in form.

Disciples Traditions

Somewhere in the hills of western Pennsylvania, during the summer of 1812, Alexander Campbell, along with his wife, mother, and father, stepped into the waters of Buffalo Creek and was immersed in baptism. The act resulted from careful study and from Campbell's conclusion that persons baptized in New Testament times were responsible believers and were immersed. By consensus rather than formal declaration, those who founded the Disciples movement rejected infant baptism and adopted immersion as the accepted form. The question of fellowship with the unimmersed was a source of controversy for a century and more. Ultimately, the moderate views of Barton Stone prevailed, with the acceptance of mutual recognition for all who are baptized into Christ and belong to the people of the one God.

Disciples believe that through baptism the church defines itself. The baptismal ceremony marks the line between the church and the world. Baptism is seen as a rite of the church that is conferred rather than chosen. The primary act is God's, and we respond through voluntary testimony of faith in Christ. In this act, the ideals of Christian community are etched into the spirit of the new Christian as inescapable responsibilities.

The sacrament of baptism assures us of the grace of God as divine love touches us personally, cleanses us of sin, relieves the burden of guilt, claims us for a new life, and ordains us to serve in Christ's name.

- Baptism is a transaction between God and the soul. It is a vital moment of consecration and covenant wherein God imparts the gift of grace. We respond with the proclamation of our faith and are baptized into Christ, committing our lives to the way of Christ.

- Baptism reenacts the death, burial, and resurrection of Christ. Through this rite, the critical events of Christ's life are incorporated into our own experience.

- Baptism purges all things that have diminished the life of our spirit. The old life is buried, new life is born, sins are forgiven. Baptism represents a clear break with the past, a moral cleansing, a transformation of the soul, a receiving of grace.

- Baptism brings us into the fellowship of the church. It identifies us as members of a congregation.

- Baptism creates a bond linking us to the whole people of God. Through this act, we become "ordained to the priesthood of all believers," a part of a new moral order, a kindred spirit with the global company of Christians.

Disciples Affirmations

Through baptism into Christ we enter into newness of life and are made one with the whole people of God.

The Design

We, the Christian Church (Disciples of Christ), confess that all who are baptized into Christ are members of His Universal Church and belong to and share in His ministry through the People of the One God.

Resolution 7560—General Assembly, 1975
"Toward the Mutual Recognition of Members"

Scriptures

In those days Jesus came from Nazareth of Galilee and was baptized by John in the Jordan. And just as he was coming up out of the water, he saw the heavens torn apart and the Spirit descending like a dove on him. And a voice came from heaven, "You are my Son, the Beloved; with you I am well pleased."

Mark 1:9–11

...all of us who have been baptized into Christ Jesus were baptized into his death....we have been buried with him by baptism into death, so that, just as Christ was raised from the dead by the glory of the Father, so we too might walk in newness of life. For if we have been united with him in a death like his, we will certainly be united with him in a resurrection like his. We know that our old self was crucified with him so that the body of sin might be destroyed, and we might no longer be enslaved to sin.

Romans 6:3–6

"Go therefore and make disciples of all nations, baptizing them in the name of the Father and of the Son and of the Holy Spirit."

Matthew 28:19

Peter said to them, "Repent, and be baptized every one of you in the name of Jesus Christ so that your sins may be forgiven; and you will receive the gift of the Holy Spirit."

Acts 2:38

There is one body and one Spirit, just as you were called to the one hope of your calling, one Lord, one faith, one baptism, one God and Father of all, who is above all and through all and in all.

Ephesians 4:4–6

Baptism...saves you—not as a removal of dirt from the body, but as an appeal to God for a good conscience, through the resurrection of Jesus Christ....

1 Peter 3:21

The Lord's Supper

General Briefing

In A.D. 54, a little community of believers at Corinth was urged by the apostle Paul to rekindle the spirit and essence of the supper instituted by Jesus. Paul's compelling description of the Lord's Supper enshrined it as the most sacred tradition of the church. Known by many names—holy communion, eucharist, Lord's Supper, Lord's Table—it is practiced across Christianity today with varying regularity and form.

Disciples Traditions

In the late spring of 1811, a little community of believers at Brush Run, urged by Thomas Campbell, rekindled the spirit and origin of the Lord's Supper. As they sought to restore the essence of the New Testament church, the practice of holy communion became the central element of worship. By mutual agreement rather than denominational edict, the Lord's Supper is offered every Sunday and on special days such as Christmas Eve and Maundy Thursday. It is administered by chosen members of the congregation, with an ordained minister normally presiding. The Lord is the host of the table and it is open to all who confess that Jesus Christ is Lord. The extraordinary significance of the Lord's Supper to Disciples is apparent in the designation of a chalice as the focal point of the denominational symbol.

Participation in the sacrament of communion, long identified as an ordinance within the Christian Church (Disciples of Christ), embraces a broad range of meaning.

• Through the sharing of bread and wine ("my body...my blood"), we meet and receive the living Christ. We affirm the presence of the living Lord and proclaim him the dominant power in our lives.

• The Lord's Supper is an act of thanksgiving for the renewal of our lives through the forgiveness of God. Through the Lord's Supper, we pledge faithfulness and reaffirm the covenant of new life into which we entered at baptism.

• The Lord's Supper is celebrated in fellowship with the whole people of God. It is an expression of unity, of oneness in Christ, and of concern for each other. We, therefore, break bread in community and feast with legions.

• The Lord's Supper is a time of self-examination, personal confession of sin, and receiving God's forgiveness.

• Through this sacrament, we remember with profound gratitude and hope the death and resurrection of Christ. We recall the sacrifice of Christ's life, and fix our hope upon the promise "until he comes."

Disciples Affirmations

At the table of the Lord we celebrate with thanksgiving the saving acts and presence of Christ.

The Design

Scriptures

While they were eating, he took a loaf of bread, and after blessing it he broke it, gave it to them, and said, "Take; this is my body." Then he took a cup, and after giving thanks he gave it to them, and all of them drank from it. He said to them, "This is my blood of the covenant, which is poured out for many. Truly I tell you, I will never again drink of the fruit of the vine until that day when I drink it new in the kingdom of God."

Mark 14:22–25

…the Lord Jesus on the night when he was betrayed took a loaf of bread, and when he had given thanks, he broke it and said, "This is my body that is for you. Do this in remembrance of me." In the same way he took the cup also, after supper, saying, "This cup is the new covenant in my blood. Do this, as often as you drink it, in remembrance of me." For as often as you eat this bread and drink the cup, you proclaim the Lord's death until he comes.

1 Corinthians 11:23–26

On the first day of the week, when we met to break bread….

Acts 20:7

They devoted themselves to the apostles' teaching and fellowship, to the breaking of bread and the prayers. Day by day, as they spent much time together in the temple, they broke bread at home and ate their food with glad and generous hearts….

Acts 2:42, 46

4

Disciples at Worship

Worship

General Briefing

The scriptures record that Abraham "moved his tent, and came and settled by the oaks of Mamre...and there he built an altar to the LORD" (Genesis 13:18). Those same scriptures record that Lot pitched his tent toward Sodom (13:12). The sharply contrasting decisions of Abraham and Lot reveal an ageless truth: To worship is a free choice.

The choice to worship has been exercised by all cultures in all ages, and the gods have been many. Throughout the epochs of human history, religious bodies have found that careful attention to acts of worship can enrich the lives of a whole people. The individual choice of placing an altar of worship at the center of life is a decisive act that carries far-reaching implications for persons and for entire civilizations.

The character of worship in New Testament times, as determined from limited evidence, was simple and unadorned. Offered in homes and on occasion in catacombs, early Christian worship consisted generally of fellowship, pro-

31

claiming the gospel, and breaking bread. With the passage of centuries, the style of worship took on the sophistication of ritual, liturgy, costume, and visual images, and was conducted in massive cathedrals by professional clergy. Reaction to this long-practiced style came from theologians who suggested that people at worship should be more than mere spectators viewing a performance, and that clergy and choirs should be thought of as prompters in the wings for the worshipers who are the actual center-stage participants. The character of worship among religious bodies today offers considerable variety, ranging from settings of elaborate high-church ritual to settings of simple and casual community gatherings, depending largely on local sociocultural preference.

Disciples Traditions

History records that Stone and the Campbells left their homes and settled in the hills where they built crude houses to the Lord. Intent upon restoring the simplicity of New Testament worship, the early Disciples and Christians were spartan in the design and construction of their church buildings and in the structure of their worship. The appearance of carpets, organs, crosses, and ornamental architectural designs was not common until the Victorian era of the late nineteenth century.

Worship services in early Disciples churches generally included periods for praising God, reading the Bible, praying, taking an offering, sharing in the Lord's Supper, and listening to a sermon. These have remained the basic ingredients of worship for Disciples throughout their history. Alexander Campbell believed that the sequence in which those worship activities occurred was not important and he therefore urged each congregation to order its worship as it chose. Rather than achieving their goal of restoring New Testament simplicity, it is more accurate to say that Disciples succeeded in adapting a Calvinist or free-church style of worship.

Some authorities suggest that modern Disciples worship contains two primary elements: the Word and the sacraments, or God speaking and humans responding. Others offer a more complete description of the Disciples style of worship that includes (1) the *adoration* of God through song, (2) a reverent expression of *thanksgiving* through prayer and offering, (3) *proclaiming* God through scripture and sermon, (4) receiving *renewal* through the sacraments, and (5) participation through *fellowship* with the whole people of God.

More than all else, congregations are communities of worship. The moment of worship touches the core of our being where all issues are joined. It is a moment when we search for the deeper meaning of God, set our purpose in perspective, and sense a transformation of the self-centeredness that frustrates our best insights and highest resolves. It is a moment that expands our souls.

Disciples Affirmations

In the bonds of Christian faith we yield ourselves to God that we may serve the One whose kingdom has no end. Blessing, glory and honor be to God forever.

The Design

Scriptures

"God is spirit, and those who worship him must worship in spirit and truth."

John 4:24

They devoted themselves to the apostles' teaching and fellowship, to the breaking of bread and the prayers.

Acts 2:42

Prayer

General Briefing

The scriptures brim with the language of prayer. The eloquence of prayer is found in the Psalms, in Job, and in the lamentations of the prophets; its perfection, in the prayers of Christ. It is the only language that expresses the full depth and breadth of our lives.

Prayer is the means through which humankind intimately relates to God. Often defined as "communion with God," prayer opens the heart and mind to receive the touch of grace, to liberate the soul from the sag of mediocrity. It is the most critical and essential experience in the life of Christian faith.

Public worship provides prayer in many forms. There are prayers of *adoration* through which God is praised and glorified. Prayers of *thanksgiving*, often spontaneous, express gratitude for the love of God given in so many ways to all people. There are prayers of *contemplation*, tranquil moments of meditation, frequently in silence, when the soul rests and reflects. Prayers of *confession* provide moments to present ourselves as we are, strength and flaw, wisdom and folly, and to submit to the truth of God. The prayers of *intercession* are given for the sake of others and reflect our appreciation of the dreams and struggles, the joy and sorrow of other people. Prayers of *petition* contain our personal request for God's blessing, a form of prayer affirmed by Christ's words, "Ask, and it will be given you" (Matthew 7:7). Supremely important are prayers of *submission*, through which we bring our wills into harmony with God's will, especially when we pray, "Your will be done" (Matthew 6:10). Through the richness of these variations of prayer, we are able to know God.

Disciples Traditions

Disciples have always viewed prayer as the major discipline of the Christian life. The emphasis has been more upon private prayer than upon a formalized public ordering of prayer in worship. It has been the way through which the privatization of faith has been perceived and practiced over the course of Disciples experience. As a means of enriching the Disciples' personal life in God's presence there has been much activity, in the publication of devotional literature such as *The Secret Place* and *Fellowship of Prayer*, the distribution of materials to assist in individual Bible study, the encouragement of family devotions, and the emphasis upon preserving private time for reflection.

The private nature of prayer among Disciples has always been supplemented with participation in public worship, keeping the private experience from descending into a sentimental self-centeredness. Listen carefully, and one will note that Disciples prayers in the public sanctuary and in the privacy of the heart are dominated by thankfulness.

Scriptures

"Pray then in this way: Our Father in heaven, hallowed be your name. Your kingdom come. Your will be done, on earth as it is in heaven. Give us this day our daily bread. And forgive us our debts, as we also have forgiven our debtors. And do not bring us to the time of trial, but rescue us from the evil one."
Matthew 6:9–13

"Two men went up to the temple to pray, one a Pharisee and the other a tax collector. The Pharisee, standing by himself, was praying thus, 'God, I thank you that I am not like other people: thieves, rogues, adulterers, or even like this tax collector. I fast twice a week; I give a tenth of all my income.' But the tax collector, standing far off, would not even look up to heaven, but was beating his breast and saying, 'God, be merciful to me, a sinner!' I tell you, this man went down to his home justified rather than the other; for all who exalt themselves will be humbled, but all who humble themselves will be exalted."
Luke 18:10–14

Seasons

General Briefing

There is a seasonal rhythm to the church year patterned after the life of Jesus Christ. The birth, death, resurrection, and ascension of Christ are celebrated at assigned periods on the calendar by most religious bodies in Christianity. Known as holy days or holy seasons, these appointed periods enrich the believers' participation in worship and enhance the understanding of Christ's centrality to the Christian faith.

Disciples Traditions

Recognition of holy days has a limited tradition among Disciples. In recent years, an increasing number of pulpits and pastors have become adorned with colored paraments and vestments to mark the arrival and passage of each holy season. Those congregations that formally celebrate the orderly progression of the Lord's life in the church year choose from among the five seasons as described in the annual planning guide of the Christian Church (Disciples of Christ).

Advent-Christmas (November-January)

Advent, meaning "coming," begins four weeks before Christmas and anticipates Bethlehem and the consummation of the promise. Christmas and the eleven days that follow celebrate the birth of Jesus, showing in human form God's love for all humanity.

Liturgical colors: *violet* for Advent, symbolizing royalty and penitence, then *white* from Christmas Eve on.

Epiphany (January-March)

Epiphany means "appearing," and recalls the visit of the Magi as well as Jesus' baptism. The season heralds the unveiling of God's gift to humankind.

Liturgical color: *white*, symbolizing purity, joy, and the light of truth.

Lent (March-April)

The Lenten season, beginning on Ash Wednesday and lasting forty weekdays up to Easter, is a time of repentance and self-examination. Lent, originally meaning "spring," is a period for church members to reflect and act on renewal, rebirth, and reconciliation with God's will.

Liturgical colors: *violet*, symbolizing royalty and penitence; *red* or *black*, only on Good Friday, symbolizing blood and darkness.

Eastertide (April-June)

This season begins with Easter and continues for seven weeks until Pentecost. It brings hope and rejoicing, along with a sense of responsibility to help alleviate injustice, exploitation, and the denial of human dignity.

Liturgical color: *white*, symbolizing purity, joy, and the light of truth.

Pentecost (June-November)

The Day of Pentecost concludes the Easter celebration. The church's birthday is commemorated fifty days after Easter, remembering the descent of the Holy Spirit on the new believers and the apostles in Jerusalem.

Liturgical color: *green*, symbolizing the life of the earth, nature, and hope.

5

Disciples and Mission

Search for Unity

General Briefing

The New Testament church was an informal fellowship of those who believed in Jesus Christ. Communities of Christians took root throughout much of the Mediterranean world, but there was no unifying structure, no uniform pattern of local organization, and no constituted order of clergy. Historical inertia had not yet carried the church through its natural growth toward organization because it had not at that moment recognized either long-range or large-scale tasks. Unity was lodged in spirit and in the lordship of Jesus Christ.

As the centuries passed, the church became increasingly institutionalized. During the sixteenth-century Protestant Reformation, the formalized church of Western Europe was displaced by a pattern of diverse national religions continuing the medieval alliance of church and state. The revolutionary political reforms of later centuries spawned the new denominational system, which was particularly adaptive to the American environment of liberty and equality.

Disciples Traditions

The ardent impulse for Christian unity has been in the bloodline of the Christian Church (Disciples of Christ) through two centuries of its lineage. The concept of unity has taken new form with each generation, evolving out of the early nineteenth-century mix of religious fragments in local communities, to a twentieth-century design of universal corporate structures, to the present quest for union embracing diversity.

With the hope of achieving peace and harmony in the communities they served, Barton Stone and Thomas Campbell sought an underlying unity of spirit and character among the disparate pieces of the church. Stone thought of himself and his followers as peacemakers, reducing denominational divisions and following the "polar star" of unity onto the common ground of Christ. Thomas Campbell condemned the "heinous nature...of religious controversy among Christians," but recognized that the church must exist in locally separate and distinct societies. In one of the most important statements in the whole history of ecumenism, Campbell offered his belief that "uncharitable division" was avoidable by accepting the principle that "the church of Christ upon earth is essentially, intentionally, and constitutionally one." The intense passion for unity often came into conflict with the more intense passion for individual expressions of faith, a conflict that has repeatedly blunted unity initiatives. The Stone-Campbell movements eventually joined in a union made possible by its localism and the elastic quality of its organization, which allowed for diversity. It was the first and last instance of union to occur in Disciples history within the United States and Canada.

The "polar star" of unity became clouded for a time during the late 1800s as the Stone-Campbell movement concentrated its energies upon the restoration of the New Testament church. The restoration effort led to divisiveness rather than unity, producing three distinct denominations.

Under the prophetic guidance of such leaders as Peter Ainslie, Charles Clayton Morrison, George G. Beazley, Jr., and Paul A. Crow, Jr., the Christian Church (Disciples of Christ) has become recognized as one of the most forceful voices in Christianity promoting ecumenical reform throughout the twentieth century. Disciples have actively related to all major conciliar structures, including the Federal Council of Churches (1908), the World Council of Churches (1948), and the National Council of Churches (1950). Currently, a Disciples minister, Reverend Joan Campbell, serves as General Secretary of the National Council. In 1910, the Disciples formed the Council on Christian Union, now the Council on Christian Unity, which was the first ecumenical agency of its kind created by a denomination to cultivate the ideal of unity.

Throughout the century, Disciples have followed the polar star into numerous conversations toward corporate union on a grand scale. These efforts have included the Philadelphia Plan (1918), the Greenwich Plan (1946-1957), conversations with American Baptists (1940s-1950s), conversations with the United Church of Christ leading to a commitment to ecumenical partnership (1961-1966, 1977, and continuing), and the most comprehensive effort of all, the Consultation on Church Union (1962 and continuing).

As we enter the closing years of the twentieth century the polar star of the Christian Church (Disciples of Christ) remains undimmed. The quest for unity proceeds as a quest refined. It is a quest for a unity through common faith in Christ, a unity of humankind, a unity in freedom, a unity that comprehends a vast diversity of beliefs, and a unity that must begin within each human soul.

Disciples Affirmations

We *will*, that this body die, be dissolved, and sink into union with the Body of Christ at large; for there is but one Body, and one Spirit, even as we are called in one hope of our calling.

The Last Will and Testament of the
Springfield Presbytery (1804)

That the church of Christ upon earth is essentially, intentionally, and constitutionally one; consisting of all those in every place that profess their faith in Christ.

Declaration and Address, 1809

Within the whole family of God on earth, the church appears wherever believers in Jesus Christ are gathered in his name.

The Design

Scriptures

"I ask not only on behalf of these, but also on behalf of those who will believe in me through their word, that they may all be one.

John 17:20

There is one body and one Spirit, just as you were called to the one hope of your calling, one Lord, one faith, one baptism, one God and Father of all, who is above all and through all and in all.

Ephesians 4:4–6

Now I appeal to you, brothers and sisters, by the name of our Lord Jesus Christ, that all of you be in agreement and that there be no divisions among you, but that you be united in the same mind and the same purpose. For it has been reported to me by Chloe's people that there are quarrels among you, my brothers and sisters. What I mean is that each of you says, "I belong to Paul," or "I belong to Apollos," or "I belong to Cephas," or "I belong to Christ." Has Christ been divided?

1 Corinthians 1:10–13

Global Mission

General Briefing

The final words of Jesus Christ to his disciples were "Go therefore and make disciples of all nations" (Matthew 28:19). Responding to this great commission, the apostles traveled their separate directions across the known world, proclaiming Christ. Their message transcended nation, race, class, and culture. All persons on earth were seen as children of God and bound together as the whole people of God through faith in Jesus Christ.

Disciples Traditions

The Stone-Campbell movement was among the leaders of Protestantism in developing a network of overseas missions. Foreign missionaries were dispatched by the movement as early as 1849. By 1918 the number of missionaries supported by the Foreign Christian Missionary Society totaled 185 persons stationed in all corners of the earth. Key leaders of that mission thrust were Caroline Neville Pearre of the Christian Woman's Board of Missions and Archibald McLean of the Foreign Christian Missionary Society.

The character of Disciples mission work during the nineteenth and early twentieth centuries was largely evangelistic and denominational. Congregations and individuals generously supported the effort by contributing funds, accepting living-link missionaries, and donating the endowment to found a College of Missions for the training of missionaries. Although the formation of the United Christian Missionary Society in 1919 combined home and overseas programs as a single mission, the character and thrust of the foreign mission segment remained substantially unchanged through World War II.

A watershed in the Disciples mission effort was reached in 1959 with the approval of a policy statement entitled

"Strategy of World Mission: Basic Policy of the Division of World Mission of the United Christian Missionary Society." This new statement was born of the reaction against the smothering effects of denominationalism, colonialism, and imperialism upon church mission. Couched in an affirmation of human dignity, freedom, and economic justice as legitimate concerns of the Christian faith, the statement declared that the mission effort should intimately relate to the life of the people by assisting in the development of indigenous forms of worship, leadership, organization, and theology. It was bold in its call to abandon the "old possessiveness" and to pursue mission in an ecumenical context with a multiform purpose of proclamation, fellowship, and service. It was the express intent of this innovative strategy to be mobile, flexible, and open-ended. This shift of mission focus was ratified by Disciples in the General Assembly in 1981.

Implementation of the new strategy transformed the character of the Disciples foreign mission program. New overseas personnel are sent not on initiative from the Christian Church (Disciples of Christ) but in response to requests from the churches in the lands where they would serve. They are selected on the basis of a specific expertise required in a particular setting and situation, placed on short-term assignment, and often financed by ecumenical pools. In 1991 the overseas staff of the Christian Church (Disciples of Christ) consisted of 103 men and women in 30 countries assigned to the following geographic areas: 40 in Asia, 27 in Latin America, 26 in Africa, and 10 in Europe. Educators comprised the largest professional group with 38, compared to 8 in church administration, 18 in community development, 7 in pastoral roles, 16 in medicine, and single appointments in a variety of other fields. Full cooperation with the United Church Board for World Ministries and the National Council of the Churches of Christ in the United States of America provides numerous channels through which the Christian Church (Disciples of Christ) participates in common global ministries.

The restructure process of the late 1960s altered the organizational character of Disciples administration of overseas ministries. The United Christian Missionary Society was converted to a holding company and two new divisions, integrally related to the church, were created: the Division of Overseas Ministries and the Division of Homeland Ministries. Through the Division of Overseas Ministries, the Christian Church (Disciples of Christ) deals directly with sister churches overseas. This church-to-church directness, as contrasted with societies to church, represents a dramatic change of relationship, a concept pioneered by Disciples. The new concept has enabled the Christian Church (Disciples of Christ) "to participate faithfully in Christ's ministry of witness, service and reconciliation in the whole world," and to renew its effort to fulfill Christ's ancient commission.

Disciples Affirmations

In Christ's name and by his grace we accept our mission of witness and service to all people.

The Design

Scriptures

"All authority in heaven and on earth has been given to me. Go therefore and make disciples of all nations, baptizing them in the name of the Father and of the Son and of the Holy Spirit, and teaching them to obey everything that I have commanded you. And remember, I am with you always, to the end of the age."

Matthew 28:18–20

"...and you will be my witnesses in Jerusalem, in all Judea and Samaria, and to the ends of the earth."

Acts 1:8

6

Disciples and Moral-Ethical Issues

Disciples Traditions

From their origins as a rural people and their belief in the sovereignty of individual choice, Disciples were slow to develop a collective social consciousness. Socially isolated and concentrating upon missionary efforts along with their own growth as a movement, they assigned lower priority to the moral-ethical questions in the society around them.

The rapid industrialization of America during the final decades of the nineteenth century spawned a wide range of social issues that awakened a new moral concern among Disciples. Among those issues were violent disputes between labor and management, the quality of life in a rapidly urbanizing society, growing classes of economically and politically oppressed persons, and a broad array of questions in the area of human and civil rights. Sensitized by these social disorders, Disciples debated whether the role of the church was to evangelize persons or to engage actively in efforts to change the social environment. Their decision was to attempt both.

Although nineteenth-century Disciples rarely spoke with one voice on controversial social questions, there was one striking exception. A major issue of that era was the manufacture and sale of liquor, which Disciples universally opposed and against which they exerted political influence wherever possible. The sensational exploits of Carry Nation brought national attention to the Disciples and to their staunch support of prohibition.

Following the 1968 adoption of the covenantal Design, the Christian Church (Disciples of Christ) had a representative means for speaking as a church and proceeded to do so regularly. In its eleven General Assemblies (1969-1989) since that time, the church has spoken more than 220 times through formal resolutions on the moral-ethical issues of the day. This accounts for nearly one third of all official actions of the church during the entire twenty years, a fact that attests to social awareness and to a willingness on the part of Disciples to use their collective voice to influence the social environment. However, these declarations never presume to speak *for* all Disciples, which is frequently misunderstood. Resolutions on moral-ethical issues call the church to study and engagement, but do not impose universally held positions on its members.

That is one aspect of Disciples' tenacity in defending the freedom of individual opinion. Hearkening back to the impetus for their own founding, Disciples are still a people quick to challenge any source of authority that does not begin with an act of individual choice. An example of this continuing Disciples tradition is illustrated in the 1975 resolution concerning the still-controversial issue of abortion. The resolution was labeled "Concerning Individual Freedom in Abortion Decisions" and contained the following resolves:

1. Affirm the principle of individual liberty, freedom of individual conscience, and sacredness of life for all persons.

2. Respect differences in religious beliefs concerning abortion and oppose, in accord with the principle of

religious liberty, any attempt to legislate a specific religious opinion or belief concerning abortion upon all Americans.

While Disciples as a body may disapprove of the general practice of abortion, they recognize a greater danger of legislating a single moral opinion for all persons, thereby abridging the freedom of individual choice. On moral-ethical questions related to personal behavior, Disciples tend to affirm and reaffirm this position, which is a cherished part of their heritage.

On the other hand, the General Assembly of the Christian Church (Disciples of Christ) frequently takes a definitive stand on matters affecting the government of the social community at large. On the question of capital punishment, the Disciples passed resolutions in 1957, 1962, 1973, and 1975 through which the church has repeatedly reaffirmed "its historic stand against capital punishment and calls upon its members to oppose attempts to legislate it."

The church, through its General Assembly, addressed a broad range of issues during the two decades from 1969 to 1989.

Subject	Number of Resolutions		
	1969-79	1981-89	Total
Christian Church Priorities	3	3	6
Biomedical Ethics	0	4	4
Charitable Contributions	0	1	1
Civil Liberties	4	0	4
Criminal Justice	4	1	5
Cults	0	1	1
Ecology, Christian Lifestyle	5	11	16
Family	9	7	16
Gun Control	2	1	3
Health Care	3	1	4
Human Rights	6	2	8
Hunger	8	2	10
Immigration, Refugees	1	7	8

International Relations	13	27	40
Labor Relations	6	2	8
Language	0	1	1
Mass Media, Television	2	0	2
Morality, Public and Private	9	6	15
Peace, War	13	19	32
Racial/Ethnic Issues	2	7	9
Sexuality	11	4	15
United Nations	2	0	2
Urbanization	1	0	1
Voluntary Services	0	2	2
Washington Disciples Office	0	1	1
Welfare Reform, Poverty	4	0	4

Discernible trends emerge, including (1) clear protection of the individual right of decision, and (2) the absence of rigid pronouncements designed to govern individual lifestyles.

The Disciples have clearly developed a social awareness and are prone to speak forthrightly on issues in the socioeconomic, political, and international arenas. On matters of personal morality, Disciples hold a deep confidence in the ability of individuals to form judgments for themselves. If you ask about the moral correctness of having an abortion, the appropriate expression of human sexuality, seeking a divorce, consuming drugs or alcohol, or participating in any number of other activities that raise questions of an ethical or moral nature, the Christian Church (Disciples of Christ) will not provide a systematic blueprint for your personal behavior. It will, however, insist that you carefully study the moral and ethical teachings of Christ and assume full moral responsibility for your personal decisions.

Disciples Affirmations

WHEREAS, many individuals, as well as the culture as a whole, are experiencing confusion concerning the goals of life and principles to guide behavior, as well as the breaking down of patterns, structures, and disciplines that have previously guided them in all aspects of life:

THEREFORE, BE IT RESOLVED, that the (Assembly) declare anew its allegiance to Jesus' summary of the law, that we love God with all our heart, soul, mind, and strength; and that we love our neighbor as ourselves; and

BE IT FURTHER RESOLVED, that the Assembly call upon the members of the Christian Church (Disciples of Christ) to reaffirm this allegiance to the divine will in their prayers, their thinking about morality and ethics, their personal behavior, their public actions, and the activities and teachings of their congregations.

Concerning Christian Morality, 1979
General Assembly Resolution 7956

Scriptures

I therefore, the prisoner in the Lord, beg you to lead a life worthy of the calling to which you have been called.
Ephesians 4:1

"Be perfect, therefore, as your heavenly Father is perfect."
Matthew 5:48

Finally, beloved, whatever is true, whatever is honorable, whatever is just, whatever is pure, whatever is pleasing, whatever is commendable, if there is any excellence and if there is anything worthy of praise, think about these things.
Philippians 4:8

He has told you, O mortal, what is good;
*   and what does the LORD require of you*
but to do justice, and to love kindness,
*   and to walk humbly with your God?*

Micah 6:8

What good is it, my brothers and sisters, if you say you have

faith but do not have works? Can faith save you? If a brother or sister is naked and lacks daily food, and one of you says to them, "Go in peace; keep warm and eat your fill," and yet you do not supply their bodily needs, what is the good of that? So faith by itself, if it has no works, is dead.

James 2:14-17

"Come, you that are blessed by my Father, inherit the kingdom prepared for you from the foundation of the world; for I was hungry and you gave me food, I was thirsty and you gave me something to drink, I was a stranger and you welcomed me, I was naked and you gave me clothing, I was sick and you took care of me, I was in prison and you visited me."

Matthew 25:34-36

7

Disciples and Church Structure

The Ministry

General Briefing

Pastoral letters of New Testament days circulated among the newly developing communities of believers urging the appointment of leaders for a "noble task." Those appointed were ordinary folk chosen from among the rank-and-file first-century Christians, and they were given various titles, including elder, deacon, and bishop. Such appointments reveal an assertion of trust in the common mind, a view reinforced by the emphasis placed upon character rather than function in the phrases of the pastoral letters.

Over the course of a century, the evolving church gradually replaced its informal ministry with a formalized order of clergy. By Medieval times the function of professional clergy had been systematized into an iron uniformity, but soon yielded to a new and broad diversification due to the explosion of church forms during the Reformation. Across Christianity

today there is the barest of consensus on four broad categories of ministerial responsibilities:

   a. Preaching and teaching
   b. Leading worship and administering sacraments
   c. Pastoral care to individuals
   d. Administering the work of the church

From denomination to denomination and from congregation to congregation, there is little agreement on the priority
of one general category of responsibilities over another. The
choice is largely dependent upon the momentary need of
each local congregation.

Disciples Traditions

Founders of the Disciples movement developed their
notions of ministry out of their disdain for formal clergy, their
distrust of authority, and their firm belief in the concept of
congregational freedom. From the authority received through
Christ, each congregation was empowered to ordain and
employ persons for pastoral leadership. Those chosen for
leadership were ordinary folk, summoned from the plough, the
village, the shop, and the mill, enjoined by compact with the local
congregation and variously referred to as messengers, elders,
deacons, or evangelists. Disciples walked the line between
clerical rule and clerical anarchy by declaring the distinction
between clergy and laity to be a matter of degree, not kind.

With passing decades the need for responsible clergy
prompted the gradual development of a professional Disciples ministry that had satisfied the requirements of a
specialized theological education and a specific set of quali-
fications for ordination. Through the process of restructure,
policies and criteria for ministry were developed for the
church as a whole. Regions authorize ordination and certify
the standing of ministers, while congregations retain the right
to call their ministers and assume the responsibility to sustain

them in faithfulness and honor. The covenant between pastor and congregation is still the conclusive and confirming factor for ministry.

Disciples Affirmations

The fundamental ministry within the church is that of Jesus Christ....By virtue of membership in the church, every Christian enters into the corporate ministry of God's people....In addition, the church recognizes an order of the ministry, set apart or ordained, under God, to equip the whole people to fulfill their corporate ministry.

The Design

By ordination the church recognizes that ordained persons, in fulfilling their calling as servants of Christ, possess the abilities, qualities and preparation needed for the performance of their assigned functions, accepts their ministry in and for the Christian Church (Disciples of Christ) and for the whole body of Christ, covenants to undergird that ministry, and grants authority to perform that ministry as a representative of the church.

...the regions and their related congregations share responsibility for ordination. Specifically assigned to the regions is the responsibility to establish procedures to evaluate applicants, admit them to candidacy, care for their nurture, authorize ordination and supervise the act of ordination.

The candidate ordinarily shall be recommended for ordination by a recognized congregation or congregations of the Christian Church (Disciples of Christ)....The service ordinarily shall take place in the congregation.

Ordained and licensed ministers who continue the authorized practice of ministry hold standing in the Order of Ministry of the Christian Church (Disciples of Christ).

Policies and Criteria for the Order of Ministry, 1977

Scriptures

The gifts he gave were that some would be apostles, some prophets, some evangelists, some pastors and teachers, to equip the saints for the work of ministry, for building up the body of Christ.

Ephesians 4:11–12

But how are they to call on one in whom they have not believed? And how are they to believe in one of whom they have never heard? And how are they to hear without someone to proclaim him? And how are they to proclaim him unless they are sent? As it is written, "How beautiful are the feet of those who bring good news!"

Romans 10:14–15

After they had appointed elders for them in each church, with prayer and fasting they entrusted them to the Lord in whom they had come to believe.

Acts 14:23

Whoever aspires to the office of bishop desires a noble task. Now a bishop must be above reproach, married only once, temperate, sensible, respectable, hospitable, an apt teacher, not a drunkard, not violent but gentle, not quarrelsome, and not a lover of money. He must manage his own household well, keeping his children submissive and respectful in every way—for if someone does not know how to manage his own household, how can he take care of God's church? He must not be a recent convert, or he may be puffed up with conceit and fall into the condemnation of the devil. Moreover, he must be well thought of by outsiders, so that he may not fall into disgrace and the snare of the devil.

1 Timothy 3:1–7

Let the elders who rule well be considered worthy of double honor, especially those who labor in preaching and teaching.
1 Timothy 5:17

The Laity

General Briefing

An emerging lay element marched with the religious awakening through Protestantism during the late eighteenth and early nineteenth centuries. Due to the separation of church and state, which brought dependence upon church membership for financial support, laypersons exerted new initiative and were accorded increasingly significant roles in the life of the church. The laity became particularly active in the Sunday school movement, the development of Bible societies, and the creation of Christian associations. So strong did laity become that some theologians referred to the development as the age of "lay Christianity." The principle of the "priesthood of all believers" suddenly moved from abstract theological discussion to a practical reality.

Disciples Traditions

The Stone-Campbell movement was born at the zenith of the awakening with its accompanying emancipation of laity. Disciples and Christians alike enshrined the principle of lay sovereignty in their congregations. Recognizing a less than slight distinction between laity and clergy, the early reformers empowered members of the congregations to administer the Lord's Supper, to teach, to preach, and to hold the primary office of elder in their congregational structure.

As national structures evolved from the search to help congregations cooperate with each other in broader purpose,

Disciples laymen and laywomen were frequently chosen to lead and to administer. Laity has maintained its position in Discipledom through the twentieth century. Local governing boards and the eldership of each congregation continue to be composed of and led by laity. The highest elective office in the Christian Church (Disciples of Christ) is the moderator, an office filled as often by laypeople as ministers, evidence that the "priesthood of all believers" is a serious matter with Disciples.

Who and how many compose the Disciples laity? While the people as a whole who compose the Christian Church (Disciples of Christ) are a bit older and a bit less cosmopolitan than the nation at large, they represent, in general, a reasonable cross section of the middle class. The 1990 statistics of the church as compiled by the Office of Research, compared with the 1990 census report of the United States offers a context in which one may discover the story of numbers. (An estimated number of young unbaptized children of Disciples parents is included, to help the comparison.)

Age Group	Disciples		U.S. Population
0-4	38,500	3.50%	7.50%
5-14	146,080	13.28%	14.03%
15-24	136,620	12.42%	15.72%
25-34	111,100	10.10%	17.80%
35-44	173,580	15.78%	14.09%
45-54	118,580	10.78%	9.55%
55-64	130,130	11.83%	9.05%
65-74	139,810	12.71%	7.26%
75-84	77,110	7.01%	3.82%
85+	28,490	2.59%	1.18%
Total	1,100,000		
Male	46.15%		48.70%
Female	53.85%		51.30%

The church is "divine in intention and human in organization," and each generation of the church becomes a contemporary incarnation. First, last and always, Disciples affirm that the church is people.

Disciples Affirmations

Within the whole family of God on earth, the church appears wherever believers in Jesus Christ are gathered in his name.

The Design

Scriptures

For just as the body is one and has many members, and all the members of the body, though many, are one body, so it is with Christ. For in the one Spirit we were all baptized into one body....Now you are the body of Christ and individually members of it.

1 Corinthians 12:12–13, 17

The Design

Disciples Traditions

The Stone-Campbell movement was rooted in an aversion to ecclesiastical authority. Early attempts at cooperation among congregations were associational in character, which limited their effectiveness in creating programs of scale and range. In the free-church tradition Disciples addressed the questions of organization in pragmatic rather than theological terms. The first twentieth-century effort to improve the organizational efficiency of Disciples was the formation of the International Convention in 1917, an association that was complemented in its work by the United Christian Missionary Society, a consolidation of six independent church agencies.

Discipledom made its most telling structural advance with the imaginative development of a covenantal *Design* rather than a formal constitution. Seeking fuller expression of the meaning of church, the theologically based *Design* provided a way for three manifestations—congregations, regions and general units—to be voluntarily joined in a covenant binding them to each other and to God. The relationship of the three manifestations is one of mutual interdependence, mutual sustenance, and mutual responsibility, with the integrity of each manifestation carefully protected. There is no pyramid of authority, no top or bottom. It is a design for *one* church, not three.

The Local Congregation

Through covenant, the Christian Church (Disciples of Christ) "manifests itself in congregations." Local congregations are organized to help each member participate in the life of the total church and to help the total church function as a whole. Within the corporate structure of the Christian Church (Disciples of Christ), each congregation enjoys specific rights and shares in specific responsibilities. Among the rights safeguarded for each congregation in *The Design* are the right to manage its own affairs, the right to own and control its own property, the right to constitute its own corporate nature and name, the right to call its own minister, the right to set its own financial policies, and the right to participate through its chosen representatives in forming the corporate judgments of the total church. Freedom is always accompanied with responsibility. Among the responsibilities cited in *The Design* for each congregation are the responsibility to administer baptism and the Lord's Supper, the responsibility to sustain its minister faithfully and with honor, the responsibility for effective stewardship in the work of the total church, and the responsibility to view the church as a universal fellowship.

The Regional Manifestation

By virtue of membership in a recognized local congregation, a Disciple also holds membership in the region where the congregation is located. There are thirty-six geographical units, called regions, within the Christian Church (Disciples of Christ), each charged with functions under the broad categories of mission and nurture. Regional *mission* responsibility includes leading in the development of a sensitive comprehension of human needs beyond the congregation, leading in the discovery of new forms of ministerial witness, and leading in the pursuit of ecumenical means to fulfill mission. Regional *nurture* responsibilities are more specific, and include certifying the standing of ministers, providing pastoral care for ministers and congregations, overseeing the process of ordination and relocation of ministers, and assisting each congregation to relate to the general manifestation.

Each region, like each congregation, reserves certain rights to itself, such as constituting its own board, by-laws, and budget; owning its own property; calling its ministerial staff; and being represented in the process of developing the corporate judgments of the total church. An accompanying map illustrates the geographic configuration of the regional manifestation of the Christian Church (Disciples of Christ).*

---

*Map provided courtesy of Division of Higher Education, Christian Church (Disciples of Christ), St. Louis, Missouri.

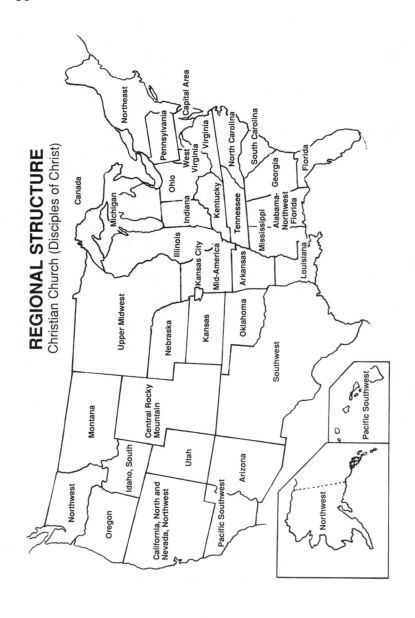

REGIONAL STRUCTURE
Christian Church (Disciples of Christ)

The General Manifestation

Each member of a local Disciples congregation is also thereby a member of the Christian Church (Disciples of Christ) as a whole, which manifests itself in the United States and Canada through a general organization called the General Assembly. This is a representative biennial gathering that reflects the wholeness and unity of the total church. Through this assembly, the Christian Church (Disciples of Christ) is enabled to speak with one voice to and for the people of the world on socioeconomic concerns and human needs, to oversee the work of the church's respective units, and to lay the basis for cooperating with other religious bodies in fulfilling a common mission of witness and service.

To inform and implement its work the General Assembly looks to its three non-salaried officers, identified as moderators; a salaried chief executive officer, designated as the general minister and president for the whole church; a general board consisting of 170 members; and eleven administrative units, each responsible for specified administrative functions, study, and service. While these components are under the general supervision of the assembly, they also function for the whole of the covenanted manifestations, the Christian Church (Disciples of Christ). The service and witness of the general church extend to congregations and regions as well as to other religious bodies and to ecumenical structures. For a graphic explanation of this unique *Design*, you will be assisted by the structure chart that follows.*

------

*Chart provided courtesy of the Office of the General Minister and President of the Christian Church (Disciples of Christ), Indianapolis, Indiana.

GENERAL STRUCTURE

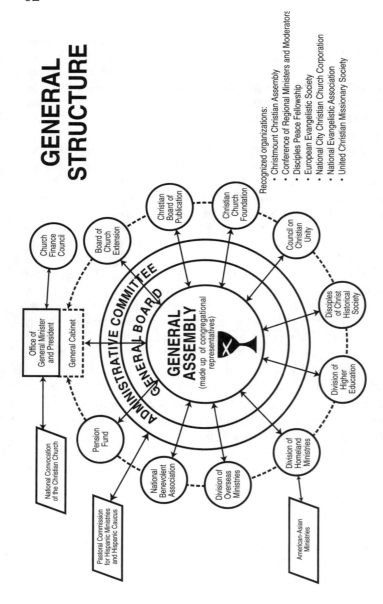

Recognized organizations:
- Christmount Christian Assembly
- Conference of Regional Ministers and Moderators
- Disciples Peace Fellowship
- European Evangelistic Society
- National City Christian Church Corporation
- National Evangelistic Association
- United Christian Missionary Society

Church Finance Council

Office of General Minister and President

General Cabinet

Board of Church Extension

Christian Board of Publication

Christian Church Foundation

Council on Christian Unity

Disciples of Christ Historical Society

Division of Higher Education

Division of Homeland Ministries

Division of Overseas Ministries

National Benevolent Association

Pension Fund

National Convocation of the Christian Church

Pastoral Commission for Hispanic Ministries and Hispanic Caucus

American-Asian Ministries

ADMINISTRATIVE COMMITTEE

GENERAL BOARD

GENERAL ASSEMBLY
(made up of congregational representatives)

CHRISTIAN CHURCH (DISCIPLES OF CHRIST)

Disciples Affirmations

As a member of the whole body of Christ, every person who is or shall become a member of a recognized congregation of the Christian Church (Disciples of Christ) thereby holds membership in the region in which that congregation is located and in the Christian Church (Disciples of Christ) in the United States and Canada.

The nature of the church, given by Christ, remains constant through the generations; yet in faithfulness to its mission it continues to adapt its structures to the needs and patterns of a changing world. All dominion in the church belongs to Jesus Christ, its Lord and head, and any exercise of authority in the church on earth stands under his judgment.

The Design

Scriptures

But speaking the truth in love, we must grow up in every way into him who is the head, into Christ, from whom the whole body, joined and knit together by every ligament with which it is equipped, as each part is working properly, promotes the body's growth in building itself up in love.

Ephesians 4:15–16

For as in one body we have many members, and not all the members have the same function, so we, who are many, are one body in Christ, and individually we are members one of another.

Romans 12:4–5

8

Disciples as Church Members

General Briefing

From the earliest New Testament days people evidenced their belief in God and their acceptance of Jesus Christ through a simple confession of faith. It was an act of commitment to faith, fellowship, witness, and service. The essence of that ancient act has remained unchanged through twenty centuries. Becoming a member of the Christian Church (Disciples of Christ) today is not unlike the New Testament experience. One is required to make a public profession of faith, be baptized, and accept the responsibility and the joy of commitment.

Disciples Traditions
The Confession of Faith

Jesus asked of the apostle Peter, "Who do you say that I am?" and Simon Peter responded, "You are the Christ, the Son of the living God." This profound confession became the model by which all generations of Christians have expressed their faith.

Like generation upon generation before, you stand alone in front of the fellowship of Disciples and listen to the ageless invitation of the pastor, "Do you believe that Jesus is the Christ, the Son of the living God, and do you accept him as Lord of your life?" With peace, firmness, and commitment, you respond, "I Do!" With that profession, your Christian life begins.

You have agreed in this act to receive the active influence of Christ in your life. You have resolved to trust in the will of Christ. Your loyalty is pledged, and henceforward Christ reigns supreme in your mind and soul.

What You May Expect from the Church

You now belong to the Christian Church (Disciples of Christ) and to the whole people of God united in a common faith. What expectations do you have of this fellowship?

The church is a company of believers. You will receive, in their presence, the grace of God through baptism. It is the place where you will receive renewal of your faith through the breaking of bread and through worship. The kindred folk of your congregation will provide a caring community that will sustain you and help you hold fast to your course. The church will be present to sanctify the critical events of your family life. It will serve as the vehicle through which you can channel your witness and service to Christ. Finally, the church will continue to educate the life of your faith through study. You, therefore, can expect much and you will receive much from your church.

What the Church May Expect from You

Disciples cherish their heritage of resistance to creedalism. Because of that heritage only one thing is absolutely demanded of all who belong, and that is to profess Jesus Christ as Lord. There are no other absolute demands.

The confession of faith is a liberating act, freeing you from the weight of false values. Your new freedom contains a different set of values, which are accompanied by expectations, ways in which you manifest your faith through the church. You cannot measure your relationship to the church in exclusively local terms. This relationship must be viewed first in the broad sense of mission through witness and service. It is expected most of all that you will minister to people wherever you find them in need, that you will love your neighbor.

Through the commitment of your confession of faith, you are expected to conduct your life with a sense of moral responsibility, to participate in the organic life of the church structure, to share in the leadership of worship, to worship regularly both corporately and privately, to be a responsible steward of all your resources, and to understand the wholeness and universal character of the church.

As a member of the Christian Church (Disciples of Christ) you will receive rich opportunities to witness and to serve Jesus Christ. Respond in faithfulness.

Disciples Affirmations

We confess that Jesus is the Christ, the Son of the living God, and proclaim him Lord and Savior of the World.

...the church manifests itself in ordered communities of disciples bound together for worship, for fellowship and for service, and in varied structures for mission, witness and mutual discipline, and for the nurture and renewal of its members.

The Design

Scriptures

Simon Peter answered, "You are the Messiah, the Son of the living God."

Matthew 16:16

For as in one body we have many members, and not all the members have the same function, so we, who are many, are one body in Christ, and individually we are members one of another.

Romans 12:4–5